THE LAST STATION

THE STORY OF DALNASPIDAL

For over a hundred years, Dalnaspidal was famous as the smallest, highest and last station to be built on the Highland Railway.

LILLIAN KING

ISBN No. 0 9530 758 1 8

Printed by A4 Print (Fife)

For my sister Isabel, who has waited twenty years for this book.

Acknowledgements

Grateful thanks to Perth Education Authority for access to School Log Books and School Board Minutes and Reports.

Published by Lillian King.

INTRODUCTION.

In "A RAILWAY CHILDHOOD", I took as a starting point the coming of the Highland Railways in the 1860s, the event which eventually was to bring us as a family to Dalnaspidal, to experience almost the last decade of its railway age. With the ending of the account of our stay there, I was left with a feeling of still unfinished business. Dalnaspidal, I wrote, had returned to its pre-railway state. But what was that state exactly? I found that I wanted, and indeed needed, to know a little more.

I did not expect to find Cromwell's armies or Bonnie Prince Charlie on my journey into Dalnaspidal's past, but there they were, appearing briefly and apparently forgotten, captured in contemporary writings. I had no thought either of finding anything of wider historical interest, having always looked on the place as belonging only to me, part of my background and shared only by a few others who had lived and loved living there. Looking through old school reports had been rather like looking down the wrong end of a telescope, seeing the child I had been. Surrounded by ancient books and dusty manuscripts, I once more experienced the feeling of being in school again, with a sense of excitement such as I had known with a new and unopened book in front of me. Here, perhaps, were treasures to be found.

What I did find was a different kind of belonging - to a wider past. I was able to see our stay in Dalnaspidal, not as an unrelated fragment of our own history but as part of the seamless web which encompassed not only the place but the country as a whole. The pattern might not always be clear, but it was there. I read through letters and accounts written by men whose stay in Dalnaspidal had been much shorter than ours, but whose thoughts and feelings had been recorded, so have achieved a kind of immortality, and at the same time, I was aware of the shadows of many others, before and since, whose passing had left no trace.

CHAPTER ONE

EARLY DAYS

The origins of Dalnaspidal are lost in the mists of time. The name is thought to have been originally Dail-an-Spideal, the place of the hospital. The First Statistical Account of Scotland says that, "here in all probability, was a house of entertainment to take the place of an inn." A house of entertainment has rather different connotations than it would have today, being originally a hostel for travellers and if one existed in Dalnaspidal there might also have been monks. Unfortunately with no evidence to support this, and the suggestion that a hospice or hospital existed here is based on the name only.

In spite of this lack of evidence, however, it is nice to suppose that there might once have been an inn of some kind close to the loch at Dalnaspidal. Thomas Pennant, in "A Tour of Scotland, 1769" says that he discovered, in many parts of the Highlands "hospices for the reception of travellers and these were called spittles or hospitals." One of the earliest maps of the area, printed in 1783 shows a settlement where the lodge and farm buildings are today and which might well have been the site of an ancient hospital.

Dalnaspidal would have been an ideal site. From Dalnacardoch, where later there was to be an inn on the stage route, the track would follow the course of the River Garry which tumbles its way through rough, barren land. The slatey grey rocks of the riverbed reflect the greyness of the skies and of the surrounding country-side. A traveller, on foot or on horseback, would welcome a place of shelter before tackling the pass through Druimuachdar - "the superior ridge" - to Dalwhinnie. For miles the track would have run through monotonous rough heather moorland and sparse dry grass till quite unexpectedly, the traveller would come upon what must have appeared an oasis in this mountain desert, a small patch of fertile land close to the shores of Loch Garry. Here is no longer what Pennant refers to as "an outrageous stream", a raging torrent which forces its way over the solid rock bed. Instead, a valley of about two miles long carries a slow meandering river where in the Autumn mornings, magnificent herds of red deer come to graze.

Because fertile spots are few and far between, this one must have attracted settlers, if not knights hospitallers, then some land-hungry Highlander who would have been tempted by the ground for grazing and planting, the fish in the river and deer on the hill. Self-sufficiency would have been possible here, and once settled, any shelter gladly welcomed by travellers. Highland hospitality traditionally demanded that no stranger be denied food and drink or a place to lay his head for the night, so the idea of a house of entertainment is based on likelihood. For a canny Highlander, the transition from providing casual shelter for travellers to using it to supplement his income would have been fairly easy.

Dalnaspidal is first mentioned in the "Atholl and Tullibardine Chronicles" which is a record of notable events in the history of the Atholl Estates, in 1669, when it's included in a list of sheals drawn up for the Earl of Atholl in April of that year. The sheals were built on the marches of the forest, "both east and west and in the middle", and foresters were appointed to keep men from Badenoch and Mar from "incroitching on my Lord's forrest",

Pennant describes sheals or bothays, as they were sometimes called, as the summer dwellings of Highland shepherds and graziers. Summers were spent on the higher slopes where grazing was possible for a few warm months, in these rough cottages made of turfs. The furniture consisted of a "couch formed of sods" to lie on, a few horn spoons and some milking utensils. In Pennant's experience, their food was often "the coagulated blood of their cattle" which was spread on their bannocks as a substitute for meat. It is possible that they bled their animals as other primitive societies did, because it's unlikely that any animals would be slaughtered during the summer grazing. The shepherds drank milk and whey, and sometimes, "by way of indulgence" whisky.

Pennant also describes the kind of person who might have made Dalnaspidal his home. The native Highlanders, he says, are very lazy unless aroused by war or other animating amusement. They're helpful to travellers, happy to give directions as to the best route to take, or to give physical help in crossing dangerous torrents, are extremely hospitable and generous, have a natural politeness, but are excessively inquisitive about the names and business of those they assisted on their way. He says nothing about their ability as soldiers but, writing just over twenty years after the ill fated 1745 rebellion, it was probably wise to gloss over that aspect of the Highland character.

Dalnaspidal played an important role in wartime, being quite strategically important and, during the Civil War, was the scene of a battle between Royalist and Cromwellian troops. The Royalist troops were led by Lieutenant-Colonel Middleton, and two Parliamentary armies by General Monk and Colonel Morgan. These planned a pincer movement, hoping to catch the Royalist forces between them. As the Roundhead troops marched through the Highlands they burned houses and crops, partly to punish the clans who had joined Middleton and partly in a scorched earth policy, to ensure that the rebels would have no provisions for the following winter. Monk, in a letter to Cromwell, says that, while they burned land where people had taken up arms against Parliament, Middleton had burned or threatened to burn land of those refusing to join his forces. The result would be, he said, that "the whole Highlands, in all probability, will be laid waste."

This particular uprising had begun in 1653 when the Earl of Glencairn received a commission from Charles II, who was of course, still in exile, to raise all the men he could for the King's service. Glencairn who seems to have been a bit of an opportunist, went to Lochearnhead where he met the Earl of Atholl and some Highland chiefs. He soon found himself at the head of an army which quickly grew to three thousand men, but Glencairn, though a good enough soldier, was not strong enough to control this motley band of followers. Fighting broke out among officers and petty chiefs who wanted to command their own men.

General Middleton, sent from Holland to take over from Glencairn, had first served in the Parliamentary army but changed allegiance. After being taken prisoner at Worcester, he had escaped from the Tower, fled abroad and become part of Charles' wandering court. Middleton hoped to augment the troops who joined Glencairn with the younger sons of Lowland nobles. It was then fairly common for families to keep all their options open, so the younger sons went off to fight for the Stuarts while the eldest stayed at home with his father to prevent their estates being forfeited if the cause was defeated.

Cromwell's General Monk saw his task to be the sealing up of the accesses to the Highlands so these cadets could not flock to Middleton's aid. He wanted to draw an impassable line between Highlands and Lowlands that could not be breached. After securing the Forth, he marched north, establishing himself first at Ruthven Castle near Kingussie, then plunging into the north Highlands, burning and destroying crops and houses.

"We have not found man, woman nor child at their homes," wrote a cornet in Monk's regiment, "all being at arms or in remote places with their cattle. At their return they will have new houses to build and corn to seek, which will be a means to quiet them."

Another troop of Roundheads under Colonel Morgan was sent to Caithness to destroy possible provisions there and hearing that Middleton had made his way into Campbell country through Blair Atholl, Monk followed him. The Royalists were forced back to Loch Rannoch and the only route open to them was by the pass that led from Loch Rannoch to Loch Garry. Middleton made his way through the pass, intending to camp all night at Loch Garry, but instead, found himself trapped. Colonel Morgan and his men, returned from their foray in the north, had marched from Ruthven where they were stationed, to Dalnaspidal, intending to camp there for the night.

It was nearly dusk when they arrived and were just about to dismount when Middleton's forces were spotted approaching on the western side of the loch. According to one of the Parliamentary soldiers they were " marching to Loughgarie to quarter, with an eye of fear backward upon the General (Monk) and being soe intent upon the waies of avoiding him", that they never noticed the welcoming party till it was too late. There could be no battle orders. There was not enough ground for troops to be drawn up, for on one hand the loch hemmed them in and on the other, the ground was all morass so that the horses were useless. The way by the lochside was so narrow that only two or three could ride abreast. Middleton had about eight hundred horsemen, and a larger number of foot soldiers a considerable way behind, but when Morgan ordered his cavalry to charge, the royalists could only retreat. Most of the men escaped, but three hundred horses, very valuable because they could not easily be replaced in the Highlands, were captured. Middleton had a narrow escape, but lost his horse in a bog. This minor skirmish marked the end of fighting in Scotland for the time and Glencairn later told his men that the King's interest in Scotland was broken "by the shameful flight at Lochgarie."

The only other things of value to be captured, apart from the horses, were some personal belongings of the Earl of Atholl, including his "Cloake, diverse letters and papers of concernement from Charles Stewart."

There may have been other battles at Dalnaspidal, but this is the only one, apparently, of which any record remains.

CHAPTER TWO.

MACDONELL OF LOCHGARRY.

For nearly a hundred years after Cromwell's troops left the Highlands, the history of Dalnaspidal disappears into the mists again. Then, in 1738, Donald MacDonell, a cousin of the chief of the Macdonalds of Glengarry, was given a grant by the Duke of Atholl, of "the feu rights of the lands of Dalnamein, Dalnacardoch, Dalanraoch, Tomickledonach and Dalnaspidal", and after taking ownership, adopted the title of "Lochgarry".

In 1741, Macdonell was anxious to join the army and wrote to the Duke asking for an "Ensigncy or Lieutenancy" in Lord Semple's newly raised Highland Regiment. He knows that nothing can be done without money and asked the Duke to make the best bargain for him, claiming it would be in Atholl's interest. "Thieving," he says,"never prevailed more than at present by reason of the last two years of scarcity." Lochgarry believed that there was no-one better suited than himself to suppress this thieving, especially if he should be posted to Dalnaspidal "about the march between Badenoch and Atholl". This place, he claims, is one of "the most centricall stations in Scotland for commanding ye peace of the Highlands", because it was the central and principal pass between Atholl, Mar, Badenoch and Rannoch.

MacDonald of Glengarry also wrote to the Duke, reminding him of the friendship that existed between their families and asking him to demonstrate this by getting something done for his cousin. Though there is no record of the Duke keeping his promise till June 1745 when Lochgarry became an ensign in the newly raised Highland regiment under Lord Loudon, MacDonell did carry out his intention of serving his lord faithfully. This is shown in a report to the Duke that he "hath behaved exceeding well in our watch". Since he began to enforce law and order, not a sixpence worth was stolen out of any part of Atholl, though fourteen herds of cattle had been taken in the hills between Angus and Lochaber.

MacDonell swore he would seize any robber that dared to pass through the hills of Atholl, and one, a most notorious thief according to reports, was imprisoned in Dunkeld. MacDonell was unpopular with bands of marauders who roamed the country, but he was not alone in his fight against lawlessness. In 1742, Lord Semple's regiment was ordered to take care of the country against thieving, and a small force of men, one sergeant and six "centinels" were posted at Dalnaspidal. That the men of the regiment left their mark in more ways than one is shown by the parish baptism register for the following year. The entry reads: "Donald McPherson, soldier in my Lord Semple's regiment and Margaret Duff, Dalnamein, had a child begotten in fornication, baptised James."

By the beginning of 1745, local gossip said that new independent Highland companies were to be raised and that MacDonell of Lochgarry was hoping to become a captain. In fact, he became a lieutenant in this new company under the Earl of Loudon, with the help of his cousin, the chief. Glengarry wrote to the Duke of Atholl, acknowledging his debt of gratitude, saying that he would "most sincerely wish the extinction of the poor family I have the honour to represent, the moment I shall be diffitient in my duty to your Grace". He also offered to give his son, Angus, to the Duke's service.

The Duke of Atholl then was James, who had inherited the title by default, as it were. His eldest brother John, the heir, was killed at Malplaquet and the succession should then have gone to the second son, William, the Marquis of Tullibardine. William, however, a lifelong devotee of the Stuart cause, had taken part in the rebellions of 1715 and 1719 and lived in exile in France until his return with Charles Edward Stuart in 1745. One of the "seven men of Moidart", William's first act on reaching Scotland was to assume his rightful title and orders were sent out for his vassals to raise "my tenants and wadsetters" to join the Prince's army.

Duke James fled to Edinburgh, and his younger brother, Lord George Murray, who was later to gain fame as the Jacobite General, decided, after much heart searching, to serve his true King. In a letter to James, he justified his decision and added that, though he had not encouraged the Athollmen, the Duke's private army, to rally to the Prince's standard, "now they are up, you will excuse me doing my best, both with them and with others".

Many clansmen who had sworn fealty to Duke James transferred their allegiance to William, and among them were Lochgarry and Angus, son of his cousin the chief. They, along with Cluny Macpherson and others who, till then, had held commissions in the King's army, became high ranking officers in Prince Charles Edward's train, and five hundred Glengarry men with Angus as their leader and MacDonell as second in command came to join the Prince's standard.
Blair Castle was prepared for the Prince's arrival and on 30th August, 1745, he arrived at Dalnacardoch, "in the mountain of Dirmochter" and reached Blair the following day. Charles's army had come by Corryarrick expecting to meet Cope's army, which had been camped at Dalwhinnie, at Garvamore, but Cope had gone to Inverness via Ruthven barracks leaving the road open. While the Prince went on to Blair, Lochgarry and others were detailed to capture the barracks at Ruthven.

One of Duke James' servants, reporting on the army's arrival at the castle was not enthusiastic about their hopes of success. He describes most of the Highlanders as "the poorest, naked-like creatures imaginable", with very few weapons. Some had swords, others guns that wouldn't fire. The "Young Gentleman" himself is described as seeming to be very good-natured, "but I do not think he hath very much in him". The servant thought it strange that, with all his travels, it was surprising that the young prince had never seen a pineapple, a delicacy brought from the gardens of Dunkeld specially for his benefit. The poor Highlanders were not so well cared for, having to make shift as best they could.

Angus Macdonald, camped at Dalwhinnie, wrote to his friend John Grant of Ballintom that he was on his way to Glengarry, "being clad with the Prince's orders to burn and harass people that does not immediatly joyn the standard." He begged Grant for at least one hundred men to avoid giving "your countrie or me any truble I doe not chuse to give."

Angus didn't go to Derby with the Prince but a number of his men did, led by Lochgarry, who by then had achieved the rank of Lieutenant Colonel in charge of the Lochgarry Regiment. In January 1746, he was, according to report one of nine officers who presented Charles with a letter pointing out to the Prince the disastrous course he was running. Ruled by inefficient favourites, Charles refused to accept advice from skilled soldiers who knew how to get the best out of their unruly Highlanders, and the retreat from Derby turned into a fiasco. Charles wanted to lay siege to Stirling Castle, a plan which the nine officers saw as foolhardy, saying that if he persisted, they could foresee only destruction. They believed that the only wise course was to retire into the Highlands for the winter, where they could easily prevent the enemy from following. In the spring it might be possible for them to raise ten thousand men, but meantime desertions were taking place on a large scale and many men were sick and unfit to fight.

The Prince refused to accept the advice of his officers and the story of subsequent events is well known, but such was the loyalty of his men that, after Culloden, his safety was seen as their most important task. Lochgarry was one of the few Highland Officers whom Charles liked and trusted so Macdonell accompanied him for much of the time the Prince spent skulking in the hills evading the Redcoat troops who were searching for him.

The Prince and his retinue moved from place to place with many narrow escapes. Hiding in a hut in Achnacarry, Charles was brought a message by Lochgarry, from the Cameron chief, Lochiel. The Chief thought the Prince would be safer with him than in Achnacarry, so Charles set out to meet him. Lochiel was then in the hills "Betwixt the braes of Atholl and Badenoch." Lochgarry accompanied Charles to "Mellanmuir in Ben Alder" where Lochiel was waiting for them, living like a lord in a bothy with "plenty of mutton newly killed, an anker of whiskie of twenty Scots pints, butter, cheese and ham."

Charles moved on from this comparative luxury to a "superlatively bad and smockie hut", then on to Cluny's cage on the slopes of Ben Alder. Lochgarry stayed there with him till news arrived of a ship to take the Prince to safety. Rather than face a charge of treason, Lochgarry also fled to France where he was later joined by his wife and children. His name was published in 1746 on a list of vassals of the Duke of Atholl who had taken part in the rebellion and whose estates were forfeited to the crown. The property was restored to his son, Colonel John MacDonell, who came back to Britain in August 1789 and, much against Lochgarry's wishes, "made his submission".

Shortly after this, the Duke of Atholl repurchased the upper portion of Glengarry including Dalnaspidal. The fifty years when MacDonell of Lochgarry held the lands of Dalnaspidal was the only time this part of the country had been out of the hands of the Dukes of Atholl until the estate was sold in 1943, after the death of the eighth Duke.

After 1789, the history of Dalnaspidal disappears again. The few papers which are available contain references to good sport there, and in 1826 an account of a severe storm. The preceding days had been very mild so no preparations were made for protecting sheep and cattle. The suddenness and ferocity of the storm was over-whelming and when it abated, leaving drifts of fifteen feet and more, squads of men, tenants and cottars, set out on a massive rescue operation. Long poles were used to probe the snow for the missing flocks and, once found, the squads worked in teams, one half digging their way down to rescue the sheep, the other making sure that snow drifts didn't cave in on them.

Throughout Atholl, Badenoch and Rannoch about ten thousand sheep were lost and "many found alive at the west end of Lochgarry can only with great difficulty be brought to places of safety." Of the Dalnaspidal flocks of about three thousand, almost twelve hundred perished. The loss was not as great as it might have been, however, because, acting under the advice of someone who had been in Iceland, the tenants "preserved the sheep under the snow, for salting the moment the search was over." They were told that the meat would look as good and be as wholesome as any prepared by a butcher, and besides, the skin and fleeces could also be saved. People, too, were lost in the snow though there is no record of anyone dying. Three of the Inverness coaches were snowed up on the same day, one at County March where only the top of the coach was visible through the snow. Although there are details in the Atholl papers of leases of Dalnaspidal lodge to shooting tenants, there is no mention of it being built. According to The National Monuments Records of Scotland the present building probably dates from around 1850 because it first appears in "Gentlemen's

Seats in Scotland" in 1853 when the tenant was a Mr. Crawford from Glasgow.

Among the many travellers who took note of Dalnaspidal was Queen Victoria, who described it as a small shooting lodge or farm, charmingly situated". Elizabeth Grant of Rothiemurchus, however in her "Memoirs of a Highland Lady", writes of a dreary journey in1812. From Dalnacardoch to Dalwhinnie, she writes, the land is bare and desolate with no sign of habitation except for "a treeless lake with a shooting box beside it". This box was probably built by McDonell in 1738 when he was keeping the peace in the hills and glens of Atholl.

CHAPTER THREE.

HOUSES ON WHEELS.

The Lodge is now completely hidden by the trees planted by the Duke of Atholl after he bought the land back from McDonell, and if Mrs. Grant had been able to travel that road fifty years or so later, she would have found a great deal more to comment on, and could even have travelled in comfort in the carriages of the new Highland Railway. By 1871, five years after the opening of Dalnaspidal station, this part of the parish was positively seething with life. There were three houses at Black Tank, others at Dalnamein and Garry Bridge, and more were in the pipeline for the workers who would come from places as far apart as Argyle, Nairn, Islay, Glasgow and Ireland. In bothies near the lodge lived two shepherds and two gamekeepers, while at the station, as well as the five-roomed house for the station master, there were three workmen's cottages. Last, but not least, there were two cottages at County March, which for some time had been a Toll Bar on the Perth To Atholl Turnpike Road. In one of these, lived a man described as a horse strapper or groom, whose job would have been to take care of travellers' horses while the owners rested after paying their road tax.

The reason of this upsurge in population was, of course, the railway. The magic of steam is difficult to define but impossible to deny, exerting a strange influence over many people. Today, when trains have become impersonal monsters without character or individuality, the continuing rise in demand for the preservation of steam engines and the growth of small private railway lines reflects not simply a feeling of nostalgia for the days of steam, but the powerful effect that railways still exercise on the imagination.

The entrepreneurs who were responsible for developing a world wide railway network were not influenced primarily by a desire to make money. Their imagination was caught and held by the excitement and adventure of driving railway lines into the heart of untouched lands. In these days of supersonic travel, it is difficult to conceive just how untouched some parts of the country were a hundred years ago. To build a railway across the Grampian Mountains was seen as a challenge of the highest magnitude, the track having to be forged through the wildest, most mountainous parts of Scotland, through an area famous for the strength and fierceness of its winter storms, and whose only inhabitants were red deer and blackfaced sheep.

Now, wherever the iron track went, so too, did the people necessary for the upkeep of the line. These people needed to be clothed, fed and sheltered, and ultimately educated, so as well as populating the Highlands, the coming of the railway would stimulate trade and industry. As well as serving the line people would use it and soon the whole of Scotland, including the Highlands would be open to everyone.

The railway companies were not the first, of course, to see the advantages of bringing civilisation to the wild areas of Perthshire and Inverness-shire. After the first Jacobite Rebellion in 1715, the government of the day recognised the need for stricter control over the wild clansmen of the north, so General Wade was entrusted with the task of building the roads and opening up this wild country so that the King's Writ might run in the whole of the land. Wade and his men found little comfort in their task and even less glory. They were navvies in uniform and for sixpence a day extra pay had to suffer the privations of loneliness, the fierceness of the climate and the unwelcoming terrain where, for miles on end, not a single tree or bush relieved the grey monotony of the mountains. The rough Highlanders were hostile, but with a largely passive hostility, showing their contempt for roads by refusing to use them, they and their cattle beating out a track parallel to that laid out so painstakingly by the Redcoat army.

Below the shadow of the bridges, laid stone on stone so that the new garrison forts could be reached more easily, the clansmen would ford the icy mountain streams rather than pass dry shod over what they saw as enemy territory. As the road continued to advance, uniformed soldiers marched easily through the land, troops of cavalry cantered by with fife and drum and the lumbering coaches of the great men, who had not supported the doomed Charles, moved slowly towards Edinburgh and civilisation.

Travelling by coach, even on these new roads, was a hazardous affair and breakdowns so common that it was customary for a wheelwright to be taken along to do on-the-spot repairs. Lord Lovat tells of one such journey in 1740. He travelled without incident as far as Aviemore then his wheelwright refused to go any further, insisting that "my chariot would go safe to London." Maybe the man had second sight for, after another breakdown, Lovat and his daughters were forced to ride bare backed to reach shelter. The rest of the journey was no better, they had so many accidents that it took twelve days to reach Edinburgh and Lovat complained bitterly about the high price he had to pay for repairs and lodgings.

He was not the only Lovat to have problems, though those of a later Chief of Fraser were not altogether connected with travelling. As an old man, he was subject to strange whims and, on a visit to his relative, Cluny MacPherson, had taken it into his head that he was a turkey hen. He made a nest of straw in his coach, filled it with eggs and large stones and sat there hatching, leaving his nest only twice a day and having his food brought to him in the coach. He could not be persuaded to give up his post till Cluny's henwife found an opportunity to throw out all the eggs and put some young chickens in their place. The noble lord, satisfied that he had accomplished his task, went about strutting and clucking in the midst of them and the coach could then be prepared for his journey home. Whether he insisted on taking his new family with him is not recorded.

This incident took place some little time after roads had been considerably improved and the Highland gentry were able to move about more freely, visiting friends and relations and when the great "houses on wheels" had ceased to alarm the inhabitants of lonely glens. Some ingenuity was used in the provision of transport. Colonel Gordon, a natural son of the Duke of Gordon, travelled to Rothiemurchus in 1809 in a boat which had been equipped with wheels. After performing the duty of a coach, it was used for loch fishing in the hills. The coming of the road probably brought extra trade to Duncan Robertson at Dalnaspidal, because in 1790, he opened a public house for the use of drovers, and flocks were allowed to shelter in his sheiling providing the pasture was paid for.

Highland roads were designed, of course, not for the comfort and convenience of the civilian population but for purely military purposes so they were unsuitable for the development of trade. Wade's roads were added to slowly, but it was not till 1802, sixty years after Lovat's unforgettable journey, that the government appointed Thomas Telford to survey new roads and improve existing highways in Scotland. Within twenty years, over a thousand miles of road and as many bridges were built, but the government then decided that roads were no longer necessary for the movement of troops, so the owners of estates through which they passed were made responsible for their upkeep. As a result, the roads especially in Perthshire, deteriorated quickly and were soon almost impassable.

They were rescued from this state by the Duke of Atholl, who arranged for John Mitchell, Telford's chief assistant, to take responsibility for their repair and restoration. Mitchell was made Chief Inspector and Superintendent of Highland Roads and Bridges, but his fame was eclipsed by that of his son, Joseph, who was appointed in John's place when he died at the age of forty five. For over eighteen years, John had travelled approximately ten thousand miles annually, regardless of weather, surveying and repairing roads. By this time, stage coaches had been introduced. With the building of the new roads, Inverness, which tended to see itself as the centre of the universe, very quickly inaugurated a mail and passenger coach service. Before then, the mail had been carried by foot or on horseback. In 1806, the first passenger carrying coach, the "Caledonia" travelled from Inverness to Perth, taking nearly three days on the journey. Guards and stage coach drivers were looked up to with respect amounting almost to awe, and arrivals and departures of stages were always occasions for sightseers.

Even in those days, the need for subsidised transport was recognised and, in 1809, Inverness Town Council furnished the money to help provide a coach, to run between Inverness and Edinburgh twice a week, a coach to leave each place, every Monday and Thursday, at seven o' clock in the morning. The passengers from Inverness were to spend the first night at Dalwhinnie, the second in Dunkeld and would reach Edinburgh on the third evening. This was an improvement on the previous time of the journey which, till then, had taken almost a week. That the burghers of Inverness already had an eye on a possible tourist trade is shown by their timetable, arranged to give "ladies and gentlemen visiting the north the opportunity of passing through the beautiful country between Dunkeld and Blair, by daylight." These coaches, slow and cumbersome as they were, linked the Highlands with the industrial districts of the Lowlands, but could play very little part in the development of trade. It needed the railway companies to do that, to cause a revolution in the life of the Highlands, bringing new life and a new people to the land.

CHAPTER FOUR.

THE RAILWAY OVER THE HILLS.

As soon as the railway engine was seen to be successful, railway systems had developed fairly quickly in the Lowlands, where there was a good measure of trade and the nature of the land made construction costs fairly low. North of the Forth, however, the relatively flat land changes, giving way to the wilder, sterner Highlands where there are large districts with little habitation and rough, rocky and mountainous country meant that construction work would not only be difficult but extremely expensive. Along the east coast towards Aberdeen, the country is similar to that in the south and this, combined with the fact that Aberdeen was within easy reach of both Dundee and Inverness, made a rail link with the city both desirable and feasible. The line from Edinburgh and Glasgow, therefore, reached Perth in 1848 and Aberdeen two years later.

Earlier, in April 1845, Joseph Mitchell had put forward his scheme for a direct line across the mountains from Inverness to Perth. At this time, railway speculation had reached its climax and no less than six hundred and twenty companies existed, with millions of pounds worth of shares being taken up by people who expected to reap enormous benefits. Many did, of course, others were not so lucky.

Mitchell, however, knew what he was about. As road surveyor, he had tramped thousands of miles throughout the Highlands and no poacher or bandit knew the hills better than he did, and his surveying experience made him confident that a railway across the Grampians was a practical proposition. Not everyone agreed with him, and these included those whose cooperation he most required, the landowners through whose land the line would run. On a visit to Lord Seafield, Mitchell was informed by his Lady that she hated railways because "they brought together such an objectionable variety of people". The estate factor told Mitchell that it would frighten away all the grouse and he feared for the jobs of the forty or so men who were employed floating timber down the Spey from his Lordship's estates. The Duke of Atholl saw dangers even in a preliminary survey.

Mitchell's proposal for a direct route was extremely bold. Much of the country to be traversed was wild and desolate, there were no towns of any size in the one hundred and twenty miles between Perth and Nairn, where the line was to link up with the Inverness and Elgin Railway. Much of the region is mountainous where narrow defiles follow the paths of rivers which are torrential in winter, or wild open country which would afford no shelter for the men who would have to carve the line out of the hostile earth, or to protect the line itself from the Arctic like conditions.

Until this time, engineers had worked on the principle that railways must be easily graded and a great deal of time and money was spent ensuring that tracks were laid where gradients were minimal. Imagine then how the suggestion of this new line would be greeted. From Nairn, it was to follow the old coach road through Glenferness, crossing the Monadhliath Mountains at an altitude of over 1300 feet, then alongside the River Dulnain to Carrbridge and Aviemore, and by the left bank of the Spey to Kingussie. From there the railway was to climb the Grampian Mountains through Druimuachdar Pass, almost 1500 feet above sea level, before descending sharply beside the River Garry to Blair Atholl, through the Pass of Killiecrankie to Perth. The advantages of a direct route regarding time and distance were obvious, but the long, steep gradients proposed were seen as insurmountable barriers.

Before a railway could be built, it was necessary for a bill to be passed by Parliament giving permission for the project. When the bill for the proposed Inverness to Perth Railway was debated in Parliament, the mountainous region to be conquered was considered to be of paramount importance. One of the opposing counsel, Mr. William Austin, during a lively debate, is recorded as saying scornfully that: "Ascending such a summit as 1480 feet is very unprecedented, and Mr. Mitchell is the greatest mountain climber I have ever heard of. He beats Napoleon outright, and quite eclipses Hannibal".

He described a book he had read of Hannibal's historic crossing of the Alps and scornfully protested that if the line should ever materialise, he was sure that "Quartos would be written about Mr. Mitchell" He went on to say that the only thing that would surprise him more than the bill being passed was that the line would actually be made. With the possible assistance of Austin's rhetoric, the bill was rejected and the plans for the railway over the hills had to be shelved for the time being. However, Austin proved as far-seeing as many another politician. While the honourable gentleman is almost totally unknown, his chief fame resting on this one speech, the name of Joseph Mitchell will remain alive as long as interest in roads and railways survive, and quartos indeed have been written about him.

In his book, "Reminiscences of My Life in the Highlands" which he wrote after his enforced retirement because of ill health, Mitchell writes not only of his involvement with roads and railways but provides a fascinating account of many aspects of life which extends over a period of sixty five years. Born in Forres in 1803, he was appointed Inspector of Highland Roads at the age of twenty three and kept the job for forty years. As well as building roads and bridges, he improved harbours from Wick to Dunbar and built around forty churches in the Highlands and Islands. He contributed papers to learned societies and was a promoter of the Caledonian Bank, founded in Inverness in 1838 and merged in the Bank of Scotland in 1907. His comments on the clearances and the effects of sheep farming are based on personal experience. In the course of his duties, as well as meeting many ordinary people, he encountered smugglers and other dubious characters and was entertained by drovers, Dukes and nobles.

Although naturally disheartened by the set back to his plans, Mitchell did not give up hope of eventually building his line across the Grampians. He published a pamphlet giving details of the calculations he had made, of the traffic he expected to result from the development of the line, the engineering expertise he could call on and last but not least, the importance to the northern counties of a railway through the Central Highlands.

It was not till some ten years later, however, that definite moves were made to renew the fight. Some of the greatest opposition came now from the Duke of Atholl, who objected in principle to all railways in the Highlands. He had opposed the original survey for the railway in 1845, when it was first proposed and his objections were still as strong. If he consented to a railway at all, it would have to be proved that it was to be beneficial to the general public, but he would not even consider it till the route had been pointed out to him and he was satisfied that it was in no way detrimental to him or his tenants. Mitchell had one thing in his favour, the friendly relationship which had earlier developed between his father and the Duke's grandfather when the road surveys were carried out.

The Duke invited Mitchell to dine at Blair Castle, and the following day, accompanied by the Duchess surveyed the route the line was to take, which had been neatly staked out with white flags. The Duchess was by far the more business-like of the two and the Duke deferred to his wife's greater understanding of the complexities of the affair. Despite the Duchess' support, Mitchell, needed all his tact and diplomacy to deal with the Duke's objections, and as the railway would cut off a corner of the park, Mitchell drew a rough sketch of a lodge which the railway would build at this point so that the railway "would be an ornament rather than an eyesore" at the north end of the estate. The lodge was later built as promised and the viaduct over the River Tilt was made much more ornate than necessary, simply because of its proximity to Blair Castle.

Mitchell made such a good impression on the Duke that he was invited to be a guest at Blair Castle whenever rail business took him into the vicinity. After his initial objections had been removed, the Duke was very enthusiastic about the project, and though very ill with cancer of the throat, he insisted on travelling on the newly finished line. On the eve of the official opening, a truck was fitted up for him, and with Mitchell and the Duchess he travelled from County March to Pitlochry. Mitchell noted that the Duke "seemed to enjoy the rapid motion of descending from the County March at the rapid rate of fifty miles an hour - rather a dangerous speed on a new made line".

But this was still in the future. In the years between the rejection of the first bill, Joseph Mitchell spent a lot of time not only gaining the support of the landowners but looking over the territory to be traversed. He re-surveyed parts where heavy work would be necessary and looked into ways of reducing costs. By 1853, there was a great deal of talk about "The Railway Over the Hills", appealing to the romantic as well as the money making aspects of the scheme. In fact, it was on this question of the "hills" that the opposers of the new railway bill, presented to Parliament in 1860, waxed most eloquent, as Austin had in 1845. The possibility of small locomotives hauling trains across wastelands, in howling gales of wind and snow, was derided. Passengers would perish in the snow and trains be lost completely. On a more practical note, it was argued that there simply was insufficient traffic to justify a new line, there was scarcely enough to keep existing lines busy.

Mitchell was wise enough to have available for his defence, eminent engineers who appear to have been more intrigued by his boldness, and by his methods of making a railway in a type of country never before penetrated, than by its actual working. The bill giving Parliamentary consent for the Perth To Inverness Railway was passed in July 1861, and in October that year, Lady Seafield performed the ceremony of cutting the first turf, chosen for this honour because the line passed through a large part of the Seafield property, and because her husband had provided substantial sums of money for the project. The ceremony was a spectacular affair.

"Into the procession every local association was impressed: the Elginshire Rifles Volunteers, the Inverness and Nairn Artillerymen, the Forres Rifle Volunteers, the Duthil Rifle Volunteers, the Inverness Rifles, the Strathspey Highlanders and the local police. The pupils of the town had their place in the line alongside the hammermen, bakers, carpenters, tailors, curriers, shoemakers, weavers, gardeners and masons, all wearing the insignia of their trade. A car with a boat on it and six seamen lumbered by. The provost, magistrates and town council, the directors of the railway, the secretary and solicitors for it, the engineer and the contractor, the inspector of the line and the contractor's agent all moved to the music of the brass bands and pipers. The navvies in their white jackets and moleskins with spades over their shoulders were conspicuous in rows of six north, south east and west of the contractor's wagon driven in tandem by four horses and containing more navvies who, under an embarrassing canopy of flowers, protected the spade and barrow that was to be used by the Countess of Seafield in cutting the turf."

Mitchell says little about the ceremony except that it was a day of rejoicing for the whole Highlands and that her Ladyship performed her duties with grace and dignity, but then he was not given to flowery statements. Furthermore, he was anxious to get on with the job and see his long awaited dream take shape.

Much of the opposition to the line across the hills had in 1845 centred around the kind of terrain to be covered, and what then appeared to be impossibly steep gradients. The advances over the next ten years in locomotive design made steeper gradients possible, but the scope of the problems facing Mitchell was still enormous, and the severest problems were concentrated in the one area with which this book is concerned. South of Newtonmore, the terrain which has for about twenty five miles, been relatively easy, suddenly encounters a steeper incline, and in an increasingly wild region the railway passes through Dalwhinnie on the left bank of the bleak and desolate Loch Ericht. There the altitude is 1174 feet above sea level and the line climbs another 319 feet in the next five miles. At the head of Druimuachdar Pass, at a height of 1484 feet, the county boundary between Perth and Inverness is crossed at what is known as the "County March" and in the seventeen miles between there and Blair Atholl, there is a descent of over one thousand feet.

The Pass provided Mitchell with a problem even worse than that of gradient. He used what he called his "morass technique" to deal with a great swampy hollow which formed part of the only possible route. To overcome this problem, first of all deep drains had to be dug to drain off surplus water, then the breadth of the line, about fifteen feet, was to be covered with two or three layers of turf, the sward side down and the bottom up, but in some places these layers had to be made twenty or thirty feet deep. Above this was laid several feet of ballast, and the railway floated on top. At first it yielded three or four inches when an engine passed over it and the rails had to be lifted and more ballast, up to twenty seven feet deep in one place, was laid before Mitchell was satisfied that the line was "all that could be desired for solidarity and permanence".

It was Mitchell's determination not to be beaten however difficult the problem, plus his enormous enthusiasm for the task in hand, that was responsible for the speed at which the task was carried out. The line across the mountains was completed in September 1863 and two years later became part of the combined operation that was to be known as The Highland Railway. The fear that had been expressed in Parliament that train loads of passengers would perish in blizzards was quickly dispersed. During the first year the line was open, there was not one single interruption to traffic because of inclement weather. In the next two years, when blockages did occur, lessons on how to deal with them were quickly learned. No less than three types of snowplough were introduced to cope with levels of snow from twelve inches to twelve feet. When snowstorms occur, they are generally accompanied by high winds so that snow quickly forms huge drifts in hollows and cuttings. To protect the line from the worst of the blast, snow fences made with sleepers were erected and though they didn't keep the line entirely clear, were effective in reducing the worst conditions to manageable proportions, for most of the time at any rate.

In the winter of 1866, the Highland Railway officials had cause to be proud because their line was kept clear while all others, not only in Scotland but in England and France as well, were blocked for several days. Though no-one actually perished, there were blizzards in plenty. In a hundred years of railway history, Druimuachdar Pass became synonymous with storms of incredible suddenness and ferocity. The speed with which a shower of snow, accompanied by gale force winds, can whip up into a zerotemperatured, howling inferno, has to be experienced before it can be appreciated. Winter comes early and stays long. The first sprinkling of snow covers the hills in September and lasts till the Gowk's Storm" in April. In July, in the hottest of summers, solid patches of snow can still be found in the deep corries and gullies.

Because Mitchell was anxious to complete his railway over the hills as quickly as possible, some of the smaller stations on the line had to make do with temporary accommodation till the more important task of track laying was complete. Thus it was that two miles south of Druimuachdar, where Mitchell's morass technique had faced its biggest challenge, and County March from where the Duke Of Atholl had enjoyed his rattling descent in an open truck, Dalnaspidal, the last and smallest station on the Highland Line was opened in 1865.

CHAPTER FIVE.

THE FIRST SCHOOL.

The coming of the railways and the growth of population led inevitably to a demand for schools. Education was always a very important part of Scottish life but, at the end of the nineteenth century, its provision became a difficult and time consuming task which for the next hundred years cost the mandarins an amount of work totally disproportionate to the numbers of children involved, and ended only when the wheel had turned full circle and there were again no children in the hills.

The history of Dalnaspidal School runs in parallel with that of the railway. Within a few years of the new line being opened, the population of this part of the parish had more than doubled, and this increase coincided with movements in the educational system. In 1872, Forster's Education Act, making education compulsory was passed, and this laid on the local authorities the necessity of providing School Boards to oversee the provision of education for all children in the area. Most parishes already had at least one school, but these were situated in centres of population.

Because of the need for railwaymen's cottages to be strung out alongside the line, it was always going to be the case that railway children would have a considerable distance to travel, and in the 1870s, the nearest school to Dalnaspidal was at Garrybridge, about four miles away, and this operated on a part-time basis. The teacher, usually a young man, was employed to teach throughout the winter months and, because there was no schoolhouse, was boarded, in rotation, by the parents of his young scholars. The school was a small building of stone and lime, with a thatched roof, and must have been very cold and uncomfortable for both pupils and teacher. The authorities were not too keen on providing another school, although there were by then about ten children of school age in Dalnaspidal and it was too far for them to walk to Garrybridge.

The School Board successfully managed to drag its heels till 1891. As well as the problems of finding suitable buildings and staff, there were the added problems of the kind of education, particularly religious education, to be offered. The two most vociferous members of the Board were ministers of the Church of Scotland and much valuable time was spent in argument. Both men had strongly opposing views on what was suitable. The Rev. Mr. McLeod wanted the Bible and Catechism to be taught "according to use and wont". The Rev. Mr. Stuart, on the other hand, totally rejected the catechism. He demanded that the children should not only be acquainted with the Bible, but should be able to repeat large portions of it off by heart, but that they should not be allowed to question or discuss anything relating to their scripture lesson.

It is perhaps worth noting, that fifty years later, though the catechism did not feature on the curriculum of Dalnaspidal school, children did, indeed, still have to learn whole chapters of the Old Testament off by heart. Ministerial wrangling continued for years, neither of them being prepared to retreat from his own entrenched position, and this tended to suppress more material problems, such as provision of a building suitable for both teachers and pupils. In 1891, accommodation of a kind had been found in Dalnaspidal, a tiny two-roomed shack belonging to the Duke of Atholl's hunting lodge. Like Glengarry, this school was to be run on a temporary basis in the winter months only, with the children being taught four or five hours on weekdays and two on Saturdays. Later, when the school year was extended to June or July, the Saturday classes were dropped.

The school was to be a Side School, not a public school, because this meant it was not necessary to employ a fully qualified teacher, and allowances could be made for the difficulties of bad weather and the availability of the school building. Because the lodge was let each year for hunting, shooting and fishing, the building was used by the tenants till October, but the actual date depended entirely on the whim of the Duke or his individual tenants.

As soon as it came into being, the school came under the control of the Scotch Education Department, as it was then, and was first inspected and the children examined in 1894. The Inspector noted that "The appearance made by these pupils does their teacher much credit". The thirteen children examined read and wrote very well and did their arithmetic very well also but "were very long about it". Their general intelligence was remarked on, as well as their proficiency in geography, history, singing and sewing. The report on the school building said that its stone walls were damp and bare, the small skylights let in insufficient light and it was hardly wind and weatherproof. Nevertheless, it was pronounced to be in "a satisfactory condition".

As well as the extended summer break, the school had two fast days, one in April, the other in October, which were linked to the twice yearly Communion Service. In common with most places in Scotland at that time, there were no Christmas holidays and New Year was the recognised break, schools closing around the twenty ninth of December. Children in Scotland regularly attended school on Good Friday and Easter Day, and it has always appeared odd to me that a nation which prided itself on its solid religious core should ignore the two most important events in the Christian calendar. From time to time, special holidays were given to mark events of national importance, either of rejoicing or mourning and the first holiday of this kind for Dalnaspidal children was the celebration of Queen Victoria's Jubilee in June 1897.

Probably of much more interest locally was the resignation of Miss Gow the schoolteacher, after ten years, because those who came after her did not have the same stamina or else could not cope with the primitive conditions, the climate or the isolation, and only a few stayed more than a month or so. It was not till the twenties and the appointment of Mrs. Davidson, that someone was found, with sufficient dedication and genuine love for the school plus the strength of character needed to survive for years in such a place. Probably one winter in Dalnaspidal was more than enough for anyone except those with very strong constitutions, and living conditions must have been exceptionally primitive. More than one teacher succumbed to illness or mental breakdown, brought about by extremes of cold and isolation, but even in such very stressful situations, no-one was allowed to leave her post unless she first arranged for a replacement. Otherwise the school would have to close and this would cause difficulties with the Education Department, who could see no reason why this school should be treated differently from any other, and insisted on the regulation number of attendances being maintained.

Although not too concerned about the comfort of their staff, Board members were very much aware of the importance of woman teachers. When they were presented with a petition from the people of Strathtummel, asking that a male teacher be appointed, the reply was that it would be a grave mistake to appoint a man. They couldn't justify the expense, because a man would have to be paid a larger salary, and besides " the children are all very young and for the teaching of young children there is no doubt that a female teacher is more effective than a man, especially for girls". They maintained that an efficient female teacher could bring boys up to the highest required standard, but the effect is rather spoiled by the addition that if a male teacher were to be employed, a female assistant would also have to be appointed to teach in what was described as "the industrial department" - the equivalent of today's

Home Economics. In fact this was later proved to be correct. The one and only time that the school had a male teacher, because the reigning schoolmistress took ill and had to leave at short notice, was also the only time in its history that Dalnaspidal had two teachers.

Young Mr. Kellock seems to have been treated rather differently than his female counterparts. Because his home was in Blair Atholl, he was given the choice of a lodging allowance or a contribution to the cost of his railway ticket. Not only that, he was given an assistant who was paid ten shillings a week. A dominie could not be expected to supervise sewing and darning, the latter skill being considered an essential part of female education. For this purpose, a wooden frame was provided, into which coarse canvas or webbing could be fitted and which was considered to be "of great assistance in the teaching of darning".

Male teachers were not expected to do any cleaning either, so perhaps it is an indication of the professional status of women teachers of small schools that they were expected to carry out menial tasks as well as their teaching obligations. The allowance, paid first in 1902, of two pounds annually for "cleaning and firelighting" the school was continued till 1920 when the first cleaner was appointed at ten pounds a year.

The School Board did not in general show understanding of the problems experienced by teachers and were less than sympathetic to a request for assistance towards the cost of piano, which the teacher had to hire because no-one in Dalnaspidal had one. This teacher, a Miss Ross, had other more serious problems. Parents complained about the way she carried out her work and it was suggested that some of the older children should go to school in Blair Atholl, travelling by rail every day. The School Inspectors were complaining, too, not about Miss Ross but about the state of the school. The Education Authority carried out an enquiry and their report said that pupils were taught in a room, belonging to a shooting lodge, which was not available for the best part of the year and which lacked any sanitation. These arrangements could hardly be considered satisfactory and they recommended that the School Board erect a "wood and iron school".

Representatives of the Education Committee eventually visited the school but their main objection was not to the shabby, cold and draughty building, but to the fact that children had to cross the railway by the level crossing to get there. They reckoned that the accommodation was quite sufficient and that a replacement could not be justified. A new school in Glenlyon, catering for only four children had cost £1350 and the committee didn't want to embark on another costly project in Dalnaspidal where, with only six pupils, " it may be desirable but not absolutely necessary".

CHAPTER SIX.

MORE BOTHER THAN IT'S WORTH.

The Board decided to defer consideration of building a new school, "as there is an element of uncertainty as to the number of children likely to attend during the coming year." There was certainly truth in this statement, which could equally well have been made at any time during the history of the school. It wasn't just the teachers who were birds of passage, staying a little while and then moving on. The population as a whole was a very fluid one, railway workers coming from all over Scotland and tending to be migratory, moving to a slightly better job or house. If there was a large family, nearness to school and station was an important aspect, and some people who had taken a job on the railway because they had been unable to find other work, were unable to cope with the climate, the terrain or the loneliness.

Dalnaspidal had its fair share of illness and epidemic, with seasons being marked by measles, mumps, chickenpox and scarlet fever. Happenings in the outside world filtered through slowly and seemed to have little effect. Though the school had been given a holiday for the Queen's Jubilee, no mention is made of her death, or of the coronation or death of her successor. In June, 1911, the new King had expressed a wish to the Secretary of State for Scotland, that children be given a week's holiday for his coronation. The School Board thought this excessive and decided that two days would be sufficient. Even the Great War seems to have gone by unnoticed except that a new map of Europe had to be drawn and the school was informed it would be provided with one "as soon as the new issue is ready." In 1926, the teacher was given instructions "enjoining strictest economy on the use of fuel on account of the present stoppage in the coal industry."

The small details of everyday routine are more important than what was going on in the world outside. As well as the new map of Europe, the Inspector suggested that a small globe would be a useful acquisition. The teacher asked for a wash hand basin, towels and soap, because without these requisites she could not get clean and tidy work from her pupils, and a fireguard, blackboard and some chalk. These were provided but a request for a grant for books was not even considered worthy of discussion. The condition of the school continued to cause concern. It was cold and dark but the Board decided that with an additional rooflight and two coats of white paint, the building would have reached a satisfactory standard.

The Board were noticeably stingy. Pupils attending elementary schools could take supplementary courses at Blair School, where the teacher was fully qualified. Requests for help with travel costs were granted only on condition that pupils pass the qualifying exam and then reviewed on a termly basis. Though few teachers could be tempted to stay long at Dalnaspidal, there was never any shortage of applicants for the vacant post. They came from all over Scotland, from the Borders, Glasgow, Ayrshire, Skye, Caithness and the Western Isles. There were no interviews, the appointment being made by scrutinising the written applications and testimonials. There was no short leet as such, but having organised the applicants in order of merit, the post was then offered to the most suitable. If she refused, either because she had found another post or simply had second thoughts, the post was offered to the second in line - and so on.

Even when an offer was accepted there were difficulties. Miss Whyte, who was the successful applicant in 1915, could not take up her post because the steamboat from her home in Taynuilt was delayed. She was probably horrified at the primitive conditions awaiting her, because soon after her arrival she was asking for items for the house she was "privileged to occupy" and which was, in fact, a corrugated iron shack. What she asked for were luxuries like curtains and linoleum for her bedroom floor, but her requests were ignored and the following year she was still begging for linoleum to stop the draughts coming through the floor, which were likely to make her ill. There is no record of her request ever being granted but she did get two rugs, a hot water bottle and a slop pail. Despite this, however, the school had to remain closed several times that year because she was ill.

Stormy weather was a factor which probably contributed to her ill health but it caused problems in administration as well. From time to time, the Scottish Education Department would make allowances for the atrocious weather and did not insist on the minimum number of attendances being maintained, but they were inconsistent in their demands, and later insisted that holidays were to be shortened and classes were again held on Saturdays. At one point, they even suggested abolishing holidays altogether and working without a break until the school achieved proper standards of attendance.

As early as 1920, strenuous efforts were being made to close the school altogether and move the children to Struan. Road transport was out of the question both by reason of expense and the impossibility of carrying on a regular service in winter. Proposals to transfer children to other schools were made at various times throughout the school's history, but if children cannot travel two miles to school, it is highly unlikely that they will be able to travel twelve or fourteen miles. As in so many situations, the people making the decisions are not always aware of the conditions applying to the area they are discussing. In 1920, the School Boards were disbanded and all schools brought under the County Education Authority, and run by what was known as the School Management Committee. This had two representatives each of the

Education Authority, of parents and the Blair Atholl Parish Council, one representative of the teaching profession and one member of the now defunct School Board. The committee was in favour of centralisation, of abolishing rural schools and conveying children to larger schools. Consultations took place with the Highland Railway Company, hoping to persuade them to renew the morning service from Inverness to Perth, so the school could be closed down and the children transferred to Struan or Blair Atholl. Of course, the children from County March and Altnagourach would still have a two mile walk to get to the station, leaving home at least an hour earlier in the morning and returning later in the evening, but that did not concern those planning the arrangements.

Fortunately, as the Railway Company was not willing to cooperate, the school was reprieved and a properly qualified teacher was appointed, promoting it from a side school to a fully fledged Public School. It takes more than a change in status, however, to change the character of such a school and the Education Department found this little place a lot more bother than it was worth. Because it was now an official school, it had to conform to the regulations and that meant that, come what may, scholars had to be in attendance at least two hundred days in the year. The Executive Officer of the Education Officer of the County of Perth had a long correspondence with His Majesty's Inspectors in Whitehall on the subject. The official letters contain a hint of desperation. "The teacher has an extended summer vacation and should be prepared to work on exceptional days, including occasional Saturdays," says one harassed official.

The teacher was willing but the little house was so isolated that "no normal person could live there in winter". She became nervous and the condition of the little schoolroom was so bad that the Duchess of Atholl arranged for the teacher to be moved into a wood and iron corrugated hut next to the farm house. Meanwhile the lodge, all twenty four rooms of it, stood empty, a fact that puzzled the officials in Whitehall. A memo added to a letter about conditions at the school reads, "I wonder why the children are taught in an outhouse when the lodge itself is empty."

The answer to that was a beautiful example of splitting hairs. "Though it is an outbuilding, it is not exactly an outhouse; it is one of a set of two or three rooms which are used as sleeping quarters for men servants when the lodge is occupied." In fact it was one bare little room and if the menservants were not housed in the lap of luxury, at least they needed only to suffer discomfort for a few weeks in the warmest time of year. The children were not so lucky. The School Inspectorate continued to put pressure on the Education Authority, because for its size, this little school was giving them a phenomenal amount of trouble. It did not, in any way, fit into their neat red-tape requirements. In the end, they put their collective foot down in 1926 when lodge tenants were still in residence on October 16th, so even before the school year began, too many attendances had been lost, and the authorities "strongly recommended" that a new school be built. It took a whole year for architect's plans to be produced and these had to be modified in deference to the climate. The school entrance and cloakroom were to face south instead of west and the roof of the bay window of the teacher's house was altered to be "such as to prevent snow or water lying thereon."

With the new school, a new era opened for Dalnaspidal children and the memories of some of those children, as well as the school's later history, are recorded in "A Railway Childhood."

CHAPTER SEVEN.

THE END OF THE LINE.

Meanwhile, the fortunes of the railway were fluctuating. Originally laid as a single line, about twenty three miles between Blair Atholl and Dalwhinnie were doubled tracked, the work beginning in 1898 and quickly bringing about an increase in passenger and goods traffic. The fishing industry was transformed, express trains taking fresh fish from north eastern fishing ports to cities like Liverpool and Manchester. The cattle and sheep trade also benefited enormously. No longer did beasts have to be herded south for wintering or to southern markets. Dalnaspidal sheep pens on the loading bank were in constant seasonal use and to give an idea of the extent of the sheep trade, in October 1890, twenty thousand animals were transported from Dalwhinnie alone. Cattle that had been driven to market along the centuries old drove roads, a journey that could take several weeks, with resulting loss in condition and body weight, now made the journey in one day.

The Royal mail also was quick to take advantage of the speed and ease of transport and the last stage coach carrying mail to Thurso ended its career in 1874. By 1910, the Highland Railway's income from conveying mails was over fifty five thousand pounds, being beaten by only seven other railway companies in Britain, and by 1913 the Highland was earning over £100,000 from both passenger and freight traffic. Much of this came from "Golf and Grouse", golfers travelling to the twenty four courses on the line being offered specially reduced fares, while the ease of access to estates meant a steady increase in sporting activities.

In the early days, passengers took their horses and carriages by train for use during their holidays, but once the motor car was in general use, that trade declined. As roads improved, toffs still sent their servants by train but travelled by road themselves, and this practice continued at least until the forties. The Highland Railway mounted a campaign to encourage people to put their cars on the train at Blair Atholl or Dalwhinnie for an easy run over Druimuachdar. " Don't trust your precious tyres to the road" said one advert.

Until the twenties, the road followed roughly the route laid out by General Wade and there was little traffic on it, but with the advent of the motor car, and especially when the gentry found that road travel was more convenient for their seasonal trips to Highland estates, a new well-surfaced road was necessary. Great swathes of new road were cut with new bridges and culverts, all of which had to be hand made as there were no mechanical diggers, everything being done in the traditional way with pick, shovel and hard labour.

Hundreds of years earlier, Dalnaspidal had been used as a camping ground for soldiers and General Wade's men had also sheltered in the little hollow in the shadow of the Boar of Badenoch and the Sow of Atholl. It was not soldiers now, but a vast army of civilian workers who set up temporary homes on the flat patch of ground where the school was later to be built. The contractors were from Rochdale in Lancashire and workmen came from all over the country, from England, the south of Scotland and from the Highlands and Islands. Fishermen when there were no silver darlings, shipyard workers suffering from the recession, from all arts and parts they came to swell Dalnaspidal's population to over four hundred.

C.C. Stuart, who had a general merchant's shop in Pitlochry, opened up a branch next to the burn and a post office was also set up, where every week, large queues of men lined up to send their wages home to wives and families. There were casual labourers, too, down and outs and tramps, but according to Bessie McBean the station master's daughter, they were all very nice and polite. There was no trouble and no crime, and though Dalnaspidal had a resident policeman for a time, the little official business he had to do leaving sufficient time for other interests, including a little light poaching on the side. Jean Macbeth, the gamekeeper's daughter, who was a pupil teacher at the school for a time, fell in love with one of the men working on the road. Her parents were horrified, believing she was destined for better things, but she went ahead and married him and emigrated to Canada.

The road took between three and four years to complete and was a godsend to Bessie who got a job as a clerkess in the contractor's office and so was able to stay at home. The only possibility of work for girls in Dalnaspidal was a few weeks at the Lodge, though usually tenants took their own staff with them. The lodge estate at that time supported no less than three gamekeepers, the head man living in the farm house, the young "gamies" in a bothy close to the level crossing. For boys, things were slightly better, there was always the chance of a start on the railway or with the new Hydro-electric workings on the big dams at Loch Garry and Loch Ericht, and later helping to place telephone wires underground, doing away with overhead wires but keeping the shortened poles as road markers to guide travellers in winter.

The influx of workers meant that there was a demand for lodgings from men who preferred the comfort of a family home to the more spartan hutted accommodation. Dalnaspidal was in great demand by tourists and by people on walking or bicycling holidays. There were also, it was said, visits from professors on botany from Glasgow University searching for a very special and unique heather which grew only on the Sow of Atholl.

The Highland Railway became part of the London Midland and Scottish Railway on 1st January, 1923. The whole railway system in Britain had been adversely affected by the war. Thousands of railway workers were killed on active service in the forces, the companies were inadequately compensated for the extra burden of work undertaken while they were under government control and services and equipment were run down. There were one hundred and twenty three railway companies in existence and the government, as early as 1916, had put forward proposals for a rationalisation scheme to reduce this to seven. With the Railway Act of August1921, four companies were formed "with a view to the reorganisation and more economical working of the railway system." The largest of these groups, The London Midland and Scottish Railway, came into being on 1st January,1923, and the Highland Railway became a component part of that vast undertaking.

Though trains continued to be worked by Highland engines, they were painted and numbered in L.M.S. livery. The provision of dining cars on some services meant that people no longer had to depend on dining rooms at Perth, Kingussie and Inverness and also meant that corridor trains had to be introduced, though a number of non-corridor trains remained part of the rolling stock for many years after.

Local trains from Perth and Inverness picked up mail and passengers at local stations and called at Dalnaspidal, though there was no mail collection there. Trains with sleeping cars operated from Kings Cross and Euston, as many as four or five a night, especially during the grouse season. With improvements in cars and motor lorries and the construction of the new north road, railway passenger and goods traffic dropped, but with the outbreak of war in 1939, everything changed. The railway link with the north was of paramount importance for the movements of troops and materials and traffic remained heavy throughout the war years. Until the 1950s, the heavier trains all had the assistance of banking engines from Blair Atholl to Dalnaspidal and Highland Railway engineers had designed a special class of engine specifically for this task. With the advent of diesel, however, there was no need for these. The construction of one hundred diesel shunting locomotives was authorised as early as 1940, and the first main line diesel trials were in 1947. The following year, the railways were nationalised, the L.M.S. ceased to exist, and before long, steam itself was being phased out. By the early sixties, plans for the withdrawal and condemnation of the total remaining stock of steam locomotives were well advanced, and this objective, gained by the end of the decade meant that in the whole area once covered by the Great North of Scotland and the Highland Railway, diesels reigned supreme.

As part of the Beeching rationalisation scheme, the double line between Blair Atholl and Dalwhinnie was reduced to single track. The Highland Railway management had early recognised that a substantial double track section was essential to time table management and to cross late running trains that would otherwise block the whole system. Diesels, according to Beeching, with their substantial reserves of power and extreme reliability made late running impossible so double tracks were unnecessary. He was proved wrong, of course, and the double track was reinstated by 1979.

By then, of course, all the railwaymen had gone from the hills. Changes in signalling meant that signal boxes disappeared and improvements in track design and construction meant an end to the need for lengthmen to provide daily care, or for the ganger to walk the line. Maintenance could be done by squads of men brought in from other areas and now even that work is likely to be done by non-railway contractors.

Almost as soon as steam was banished from our main line railways, a movement for preservation began. The Highland Railway Society keeps the Line's history alive and the Transport Museum in Kelvin hall, in Glasgow has on display a magnificent Highland Railway engine in its original livery. Railway Preservation Societies now abound and one of these is the Strathspey Railway, based at Boat of Garten, which organises steam excursions on a regular basis and serves a thriving tourist industry. Dalnaspidal station closed on 3rd May, 1965, the buildings were dismantled some time later and eventually rebuilt as the Strathspey Railway's station premises, so they at least have a future of a kind.

In 1980, steam came back to Dalnaspidal in the unlikely shape of an A4 Pacific engine, John Cameron's "Union of South Africa" and a picture in the 1986 "Steam Railway" magazine shows the Scottish Railway Preservation Society engine "Maude" climbing Druimuachdar Summit en route for a British Rail open day at Inverness.

Though endless streams of traffic swirl past along the new A9, few people see beyond the cuttings and embankments. As young children, we searched among the heather for traces of the old Wade's road that had not been incorporated into the new tarmacadamed surfaces. Very few of those traces still remain, but below the new road to Druimuachdar, stretches of two other earlier roads exist. One from Dalnaspidal, leads only to the ruins of County March and the other, even shorter, lies below the railway line close to the river. Dalnaspidal really has gone back almost to its pre-railway state, except that the iron track remains and the tiny community now consists of the farmstead, lodge and school and tucked in close to the railway line, the tiny home of Norman Alderman, who was a signalman at the station for many years. The clusters of cottages at BlackTank, Altnagourach, and Garrybridge have all disappeared. All that remains of the County March is a mess of broken bricks and roof timbers. The station cottages, sold back to the landowners, have been boarded up and deserted for thirty years. However, there is a ray of hope that they will survive. Changes in land ownership has heralded a change of outlook and the houses may soon be sold, but perhaps it is already too late. Thirty years of dereliction means that vast amounts of money and time will be necessary to bring the houses back to habitable standards, but at least there is a possibility of life returning at last.

With the building of the new road, changes to the landscape include plantings of mixed woodlands, bringing trees back to the land for the first time since it was laid bare by armies of the sixteenth and seventeenth centuries. Perhaps one day there may be children playing among these trees or wandering on the hills again, but until then, blaeberries and cranberries grow unmolested and winter mornings will not hear the sound of voices echoing through the valley.

The memories and experiences of the children who lived in Dalnaspidal, and whose story is told in "A Railway Childhood" will take their place in history alongside Cromwell's troops and the men of Lochgarry. The gulf that exists between my childhood and that of my children and grandchildren is enormous and soon the age of steam will be ancient history, but for us, it was our life and we are proud to have been a part of it.

48

BIBLIOGRAPHY.

Chronicles Of The Atholl and Tullibardine Papers, BallantynePress 1908.

The Lockhart Papers, George Lockhart of Carnwath, Wm. Anderson, London 1817.

A Tour of Scotland 1769, Thomas Pennant, Benjamin White, London 1776.

Memoirs of a Highland Lady, Elizabeth Grant of Rothiemurchus, John Murray, Albemarle Library, 1898.

History of the Commonwealth and Protectorate, S.R.Gardiner, Longmans Green, 1894.

Military Memoirs of the Great Civil War, Constable & Co., Edinburgh 1822

Letters From Roundhead Officers From Scotland, Bannatyne Club,1856.

The Iron Track Through the Highlands, J.E.C. Highland News Ltd., Inverness, c 1914.

Reminiscences of My life in the Highlands, Joseph Mitchell,1883.

Margaret Ogilvy, by her Son, J.M. Barrie, Hodder &Stoughton, London, 1897.

The Railways of Scotland, W.M. Acworth, John Murray, London,1890.

L.M.S. 150. The London, Midland and Scottish Railway, A Century of Progress, Patrick Whitehouse and David St. John Thomas, David & Charles, 1987.

National Census Returns 1841-1891, Dalnaspidal School Log Book.

School Board Minute Books, Parish Records of Blair Atholl, British Railways Magazine, Railway News, Railway Observer, Steam Railway.